CONTENTS

HOW TO USE THIS GUIDE

SCOPE AND SEQUENCE

Welcome to the *40 Days Through the Book* study on Philippians! During the course of the next six weeks, you and your fellow group members will embark on an in-depth exploration of the apostle Paul's message to the believers in that part of the Mediterranean world. During this study, you will learn approximately when he wrote the book, the audience for whom he wrote, and the background and context in which it was written. But, more importantly, through the teaching by Mark Batterson, you will explore the key themes that Paul relates in Philippians—and how they relate to you today.

SESSION OUTLINE

The 40 Days Through the Word video study is designed to be experienced in a group setting (such as a Bible study, Sunday school class, or small group gathering) and also as an individual study. Each session begins with an introduction reading and question. You will then watch a video with Mark Batterson, which can be accessed via the streaming code found on the inside front cover. There is an outline provided in the guide for you to take notes and gather your reflections as you watch the video.

Next, you will engage in a time of directed discussion, review the memory verses for the week, and then close each session with a time of personal reflection and prayer. (Note that if your group is larger, you may wish to watch the videos together and then break into smaller groups of four to six people, to ensure that everyone has time to participate in discussions.)

40-DAY JOURNEY

What is truly unique about this study, and all of the other studies in the *40 Days Through the Book* series, are the daily learning resources that will lead you into a deeper engagement with the text. Each week, you will be given a set of daily readings, with accompanying reflection questions, to help you explore the material that you covered during your group time.

The first day's reading will focus on the key verse to memorize for the week. In the other weekly readings, you will be invited to read a passage from Philippians, reflect on the text, and then respond with some guided journal questions. On the final day, you will review the key verse again and recite it from memory. As you work through the six weeks' worth of material in this section, you will read (and, in some cases, reread) the entire book of Philippians.

Now, you may be wondering why you will be doing this over the course of *forty* days. Certainly, there is nothing special about that number. But there is something biblical about it. In the Bible, the number forty typically designates a time of *testing.* The great flood in Noah's time lasted for forty days. Moses lived forty years in Egypt and another forty years in the desert before he led God's people. He spent forty days on Mount Sinai receiving God's laws and sent spies, for forty days, to investigate the land of Canaan. Later, God sent the prophet Jonah to warn ancient Nineveh, for forty days, that its destruction would come because of the people's sins.

Even more critically, in the New Testament we read that Jesus spent forty days in the wilderness, fasting and praying. It marked a critical transition point in his ministry—the place where he set about to fulfill the mission that God had intended. During this time Jesus was tested relentlessly by the enemy . . . and prevailed. When he returned to Galilee, he was a different person than the man who had entered into the wilderness forty days before. The same will be true for you as you commit to this forty-day journey through Philippians.

GROUP FACILITATION

You and your fellow group members should have your own copy of this study guide. Not only will this help you engage when your group is meeting, but it will also allow you to fully enter into the *40 Days* learning experience. Keep in mind the video, questions, and activities are simply tools to help you engage with the session. The real power and life-transformation will come as you dig into the Scriptures and seek to live out the truths you learn along the way.

Finally, you will need to appoint a leader or facilitator for the group who is responsible for starting the video teaching and for keeping track of time during discussions and activities. Leaders may also read questions aloud and monitor discussions, prompting participants to respond and ensuring that everyone has the opportunity to participate. For more thorough instructions on this role, see the Leader's Guide included at the back of this book.

INTRODUCTION

PHILIPPIANS

AUTHOR, DATE, AND LOCATION

The apostle Paul wrote to the church in Philippi between
AD 60 and 62. He was a prisoner and chained to a Roman
guard. In this dark and discouraging place Paul's joy was
not extinguished but continued to burn bright. The city of
Philippi took its name from Philip II of Macedon, father of
Alexander the Great. It was one of his military strongholds
in northern Greece. Fast-forward a few hundred years, and
Philippi was conquered by the Romans in 31 BC. So, Paul is
writing to Roman citizens. They spoke the Latin language.
They wore Roman dress. Their coins had Roman inscrip-
tions. The city itself was patterned after Rome, and it sat
on the Via Egnatia, which was a major military road in the
Roman Empire.

Philippi had a wide variety of religious influences. There
were altars to Greek gods. Archaeologists have found sanctuar-
ies to the Egyptian gods Iris and Serapis. And, of course, there

were monuments to the Caesars. The Imperial Cult, as it was called, was the official state religion. There was also a Jewish community that lived in Philippi. It was to these Christians in this pluralistic and secular environment that Paul wrote a letter of unparalleled joy.

THE BIG PICTURE

Just four chapters, 104 verses, and Paul mentions his Savior more than forty times. Every theme and truth found in Philippians is saturated in the presence and power of Jesus. It is in this book that we find the great Christ hymn that gives a vision of Jesus' incarnation, humiliation, sacrifice, and ultimate glorification. Joy is everywhere in the book of Philippians, and that is because Jesus is present in all places, even in persecution. While incarcerated and chained, Paul's heart is free, and he can rejoice.

History does seem to repeat itself. When Paul came to the city of Philippi his plan was to proclaim the gospel and lift up Jesus as the Messiah. After sharing the good news with a group of women outside the city along a river, a businesswoman named Lydia came to faith in the Savior and was baptized along with many members of her family (Acts 16:11–15). After being taunted by a demon-possessed woman for many days, Paul cast out the evil spirit, which led to a major uproar in the city (Acts 16:16–24). The Roman leaders responded swiftly and severely. Paul and his ministry team were all publicly stripped, beaten with rods, severely flogged, put in prison, thrown in the inner cell, and fastened in the stocks.

At midnight the other prisoners and the guard were treated to a worship concert and prayer meeting. In a shocking and reflexive act of faith, Paul and his companions burst into songs of praise and prayers of adoration. Joy and music filled the prison! These bruised and battered Christians were not cursing God, government, or guards through clenched teeth. They were celebrating the grace of Jesus with open mouths and hearts.

When Paul wrote the letter to the Philippians, he was in jail again. He was rejoicing again. He was willingly suffering with a smile on his face, prayers on his lips, and a song in his heart. History was repeating itself.

EPIC THEMES

There are several themes in Philippians that are worthy of our focus. These include:

- **Love-filled prayer.** The recipients of this letter are not strangers but friends, family, beloved partners in the gospel. You can feel Paul's affection for these people all through this prayer and the whole letter (see Philippians 1:1–11).

- **Evangelistic hopefulness.** Paul actually finds joy in the fact that his unfair incarceration has given him an up-close chance to share Jesus with each and every guard to whom he was chained. Before you knew it, the whole palace guard knew Paul's story and the story of Jesus (see Philippians 1:12–26).

- **The humility and exaltation of Jesus.** In one of the first recorded hymns of the early church we see the willing heart of Jesus to leave glory, live perfectly, die sacrificially, and rise in victory. Because of this, every knee will bow to him and every tongue in all creation declare that Jesus is Lord (see Philippians 2:1–11).

- **When we know Jesus, we are transformed.** Paul calls all followers of the Savior to grow in faith, adjust their attitudes, and walk in holiness. To help us have a picture of what this can look like, we get snapshots of two faithful and humble servants: Timothy and Epaphroditus (see Philippians 2:12–30).

- **A contrast of human righteousness and the righteousness of Jesus.** Legalism and trust in human religious devotion is always a temptation, but Paul teaches us that this is all garbage compared to the cleansing and glorious grace of Jesus (see Philippians 3).

- **Keep your eyes on Jesus**. How do you resolve conflicts? How do you stay joyful in hard times? How do you keep keeping on when you are weary? The answer to all three of these questions is: keep your eyes and focus locked firmly on Jesus (see Philippians 4:1–9).

- **Contentment and a generous heart grow out of a love for Jesus.** The transformational power of our Lord will change us at the deepest level . . . even the temptation to be possessed by possessions can be overcome by the power of our risen Lord (see Philippians 4:10–20).

The heartbeat of Philippians is for believers to have a Jesus-centered vision of life. How do we find joy in all of life's ups and downs? Jesus! How do we grow in contentment and generosity? Jesus! How do we grow in contentment and generosity? Jesus! Where should our focus be so that our life makes sense? Jesus! Perhaps these words from the prayer of Saint Patrick summarize it best: "Christ with me, Christ before me, Christ behind me, Christ in me . . . Christ when I lie down . . . Christ when I arise."

A LOVE LETTER

PHILIPPIANS 1:1–8

As followers of Jesus, we have heard the call to love God with all that is in us and to love our neighbors as ourselves. In this letter, we get a vision of how we should feel about other followers of Jesus and how we should express these feelings openly to them.

WELCOME

All throughout history, people have been writing love letters in an attempt to express the passions of their heart. But a few notable examples stand out above the rest. As a young military officer, Napoleon Bonaparte met Josephine in 1795 and fell in love with her. He wrote letters to her while he was at war, though she rarely wrote back to him. In one of these notes, he stated, "A few days ago I thought I loved you; but since I last saw you, I feel I love you a thousand times more. All the time I have known you, I adore you more each day."

Ludwig van Beethoven was a famous German composer who works rank among the most performed in all of classic music. He first began writing music in 1802 and continued to compose works until his death in 1827—even in spite of increasing deafness. Beethoven's passion rang out in his music, but as it turns out, he could be passionate in his words as well. After his death, an unsent love letter was found among his papers in which he expressed these sentiments: "My thoughts rush to you, my immortal beloved, now and then joyfully, then again sadly, waiting to know whether Fate will hear our prayer—to face life I must live altogether with you or never see you." The intended recipient of this letter remains a mystery.

But the most famous love letter of them all is found in the Bible. The book known simply as the "Song of Songs" is a passionate dialogue between a man and his beloved. In one section of the letter, the man uses this descriptive language to describe his beloved: "How beautiful you are, my darling! Oh, how beautiful! Your eyes behind your veil are doves. Your hair is like a flock of goats descending from the hills of Gilead. Your teeth are like a flock of sheep just shorn, coming up from the washing. each has its twin; not one of them is alone" (4:1-2).

The book of Philippians is also an ancient love letter. But it is not a letter between a man and a woman. Rather, it is a letter sent from the heart of God to his church, his people, his bride. The words are inspired through the apostle Paul to the church in the city of Philippi. But the words of this letter are clearly a message from the heart of God to his beloved . . . to you and me.

SHARE

Who is a person God has placed in your life that you have deep and sincere affection for (other than people in your small group)? What have you experienced together that has forged this kind of rich relationship?

WATCH

Play the video for session one (see the streaming video access provided on the inside front cover). As you watch, use the following outline to record any thoughts, questions, or key points that stand out to you.

The setting and the writer of Philippians

Hermeneutics is the science of interpreting Scripture (Pardes)

Peshat . . . Simple, plain, devotional Bible reading

Remez . . . Cues and clues in the text of Scripture

Deresh . . . Connecting the dots as we interpret Scripture

Sod . . . When the Holy Spirit speaks to us through Scripture

The when, where, and who of Philippians (Philippians 1:1–2)

A Love Letter (Philippians 1:3–8)

God closes one door and opens another (Acts 16:6–25)

Responding to hardship . . . whining or worship?

A serious challenge: Prophecy your praise . . . praise God
before he does it

DISCUSS

Take a few minutes with your group members to discuss what
you just watched and explore these concepts in Scripture.
Use the following questions to help guide your discussion.

I. What impacted you the most as you watched Mark's teaching on Philippians 1 and Acts 16?

2. Some people regurgitate what they hear from culture,
media, and society. They act like a thermometer that reflects
the world around them. Others declare the revelation of
God and, like a thermostat, they raise the temperature and
change the environment, the conversation, and sometimes
the world. What do Christians sound like when we are simply
regurgitating the prevailing voices of our culture? What will
we sound like when we are articulating the timely revelation
of God's Word in a bold and transformational way?

3. **Read Philippians 1:3–8.** What do we learn about Paul's relationship with the believers in the city of Philippi from this passage? As you think about the Christian community where God has placed you, what can you thank God for about this body of believers (God's church)? What are ways you can show affection and love to the members of your church?

4. **Read Acts 16:6–10.** Tell about a time you had your plans and future all laid out and God surprised you with a whole different agenda. How did you see God work through this process? How did God bring glory to himself (and blessing to you) through his divine change of your plans?

5. **Read Acts 16:16–18.** Mark talks about how the enemy of our soul wants to dominate and control our lives, and that we must exercise spiritual authority and fight back. What are ways we can resist, push back, and overcome the entice-ments and work of the enemy? Tell about a time you did this and saw God win a battle.

6. When times of hardship, suffering, or loss hit our lives, what are some of the very real ways (good or bad) we respond? What do you learn from the response of Paul, and how can you follow his example?

MEMORIZE

Each session, you will be given a key verse (or verses) from the passage covered in the video teaching to memorize. This week, your memory verses are Philippians 1:3–4:

> *I thank my God every time I remember you. In all my prayers for all of you, I always pray with joy . . .*

Have everyone recite these verses out loud. Ask for any volunteers who would like to say the verses from memory.

RESPOND

Paul's relationship with God's people in the city of Philippi was forged through struggles, pain, public turmoil, and partnership in ministry. Why is it that some of our deepest and longest lasting relationships have included times in the furnace of life together? How did God forge a deep relationship between Paul and the Philippian Christians through difficult and painful times?

PRAY

Close your group time by praying in any of the following directions:

- Thank God for the people he has placed in your life who you love deeply and for whom you have sincere affection. Ask for God's blessing on their lives.
- Pray for courage to learn from the apostle Paul's example so that you can express your love and appreciation for the people God has placed in your life.
- If you, or someone in your group, are in the middle of a spiritual battle, pray for God's victory, for awareness of the tactics of the enemy, and for the power of the Holy Spirit to be unleashed.

SESSION ONE

Reflect on the material you have covered in this session by engaging in the following between-session learning resources. Each week, you will begin by reviewing the key verse(s) to memorize for the session. During the next five days, you will have an opportunity to read a portion of Philippians, reflect on what you learn, respond by taking action, journal some of your insights, and pray about what God has taught you. Finally, the last day, you will review the key verse(s) and reflect on what you have learned for the week.

DAY 1

Memorize: Begin this week's personal study by reciting Philippians 1:3–4:

> *I thank my God every time I remember you. In all my prayers for all of you, I always pray with joy . . .*

Now try to say these verses from memory.

Reflect: There is power in our memories. Think back over your time being part of God's family. In particular, reflect on good memories, kind people, meaningful sermons, and life-impacting moments. Thank God for the people in the family of God who have been a blessing in your life. If you want to go one step deeper, send one or more of these people an email, text, or letter expressing a memory of them that is meaningful to you.

DAY 2

Read: Philippians 1 and take time to focus on Philippians 1:1–2.

Reflect: What comes to your mind when you look at yourself in a mirror first thing in the morning? Try this on for size. "I am a saint. I am a holy one of God." This is not what most of us think when we reflect on who we are at the start of the day or when we put our head on the pillow at night. But it's true! The apostle Paul refers to the people of God in the city of Philippi as "God's holy people." Another way to say this is, "God's saints." Through Jesus Christ and his sacrifice for our sins, we are cleansed and made holy. Amazing! Take time this week and try to see yourself through the eyes and finished work of Jesus. Be reminded that the holy God of heaven looks at you and sees one of his saints. Believe it and grow into that reality.

Journal:

- Why do I have a hard time seeing myself as one of God's "holy people"?
- How I can grow in seeing myself as a saint of God (i.e., how can I adjust my words, attitudes, and actions to reflect this spiritual reality)?

Pray: Praise God for his holiness and ask for the power of his Spirit to help you embrace who you are in Jesus as you seek to become more like your Lord.

DAY 3

Read: Philippians 2 and Philippians 1:1–2.

Reflect: Grace and peace. What beautiful and powerful words! What a greeting! Paul not only used these words to begin his letter to the church, but he sought to bring peace wherever he went and extend grace to each person he met. What are ways you can bring peace to the people you encounter in your neighborhood, workplace, church, and everywhere you go? How can you bear the grace of Jesus as you interact with believers and with people who do not yet follow him?

Journal:

- What are places and situations you will enter this week that really need peace? How can you be sure to bring peace and not more tension and turmoil?
- In our graceless world, people hunger for signs of kindness, goodness, and grace. Consider someone you will encounter this week who needs a touch of grace? How can you bring the grace of Jesus into this situation?

Pray: Ask God to bring reminders to you throughout this week of how you can bear his peace and grace wherever you go.

DAY 4

Read: Philippians 3 and Philippians 1:6.

Reflect: There are two truths that Paul unveils in Philippians 1:6. First, God is at work in you. The Maker of heaven and earth is intimately involved in your life. He is close and active. He has a plan for your life. Second, God is not done growing you. He will bring his work to completion, but you are still on the journey. You can receive these truths with joy and confidence:

God is near and working in me. God will accomplish his purposes and plans in me. What is God doing in you today and how can you partner in his wise and good plan?

Journal:
- What are ways that God has been working in you, growing you, and making you more like Jesus?
- How can you partner with God to keep taking steps forward in these areas of growth?

Pray: Ask for courage and power to keep taking steps forward in God's will for your life. Ask the Spirit to show you if there is a place of needed growth where you are stalled and need to begin pressing forward today.

DAY 5

Read: Philippians 4 and Philippians 1:7.

Reflect: Love is never chained. Though Paul was in chains, he still felt deep affection for his friends in Philippi and communicated his love to them in this letter. He was incarcerated because he confidently followed Jesus and boldly proclaimed the gospel. But even from jail Paul wrote words, inspired by the Holy Spirit, that lavished God's people with love from heaven. When we feel confined, trapped, and bound up, we can still receive, enjoy, and share the love of God. What can you learn from Paul's example of being chained but still free to share the love of Jesus?

Journal:
- What situations and circumstances in life tend to bind you up and keep you from expressing love and care for others?
- How can you continue speaking and showing love no matter what life circumstances come your way?

Pray: Ask God to help you speak words of love and take actions that reveal the love of Jesus, no matter how hard your life becomes.

DAY 6

Read: Philippians 1:8.

Reflect: The affection of Jesus. What an amazing idea! Paul's longing for the Christians in Philippi was straight from the heart of the Savior. What do we do when our energy runs low and our heart becomes a bit calloused? How do we live for Jesus when our body is tired, our schedule jam-packed, and we are feeling weary? In those moments (and they come for all of us) we live and love in the power of Jesus. Have you ever asked Jesus to grow your love and longing for other people? Have you dared to say, "Jesus, make your longing my longing—make my heart and love like yours"? These are powerful prayers. Dare to lift them up today.

Journal:
- Where has your love grown cold and your heart become calloused?
- How can you walk closer to Jesus so that your heart will become more and more like his?

Pray: Dare to pray that the heart, love, and longing of Jesus would flood your life so that you will look and live more like the Savior.

DAY 7

Memorize: Conclude this week's personal study by again reciting Philippians 1:3–4:

> *³ I thank my God every time I remember you. ⁴ In all my prayers for all of you, I always pray with joy . . .*

Reflect: There is power in joyful prayers. These can be prayers of praise to God, supplication for the needs of others, or thanksgiving for God's goodness. As you lift your heart in prayer, be sure you are not getting into such a routine that you say the words, but your passion is waning. Pray for joy to fill you to overflowing and for your prayers to be filled with passionate celebration. What is the joy level of your prayers and how can you increase it for the glory of Jesus?

THERE YOU ARE

PHILIPPIANS 1:9-26

There are two kinds of people in the world. Some say, "Here I am," and focus on themselves. Others say, "There you are," and joyfully love and serve others. Paul gives us a vison of a life lived for the sake of Jesus and others—a path that allows us to live as a people who declare, "There you are!"

WELCOME

Almost everything we do can become a tribute to ourselves, or it can be an act of grace toward others. The decision is up to us. From the simplest of daily activities to the most sacred practices, if we are not careful, we can become self-serving.

How we eat pizza can scream, "Here I am," or gently affirm, "There you are." Imagine sitting at a table with a group of friends at your favorite pizzeria. After a leisurely dinner and time of conversation, you look and notice one is slice left. Pause right now and imagine two options. "Here I am!" and with cobra-like reflexes you snag the last slice and gobble it down. Or, "There you are!" as you let everyone know there is one more slice and someone else should enjoy it.

When we walk into a room, we can make a decision. Will my main concern and focus be, "Who will notice me? Can I network with someone important? Where's the best seat?" All of these attitudes declare, "Here I am." We could also enter a room with a dramatically different perspective. Our attitude could be, "Who can I serve? Is anyone being left out? How could I make someone feel at home?" This kind of thinking leads to a whole different experience. It says, "There you are."

Jesus addressed this very issue around some of the most sacred of practices in the life of his followers. Some people pray with a focus on impressing others, saying the right words, and putting on a top-notch spiritual show. "Here I am God, world, church!" Jesus was not a fan of this approach. In a similar way, our Lord talked about the practice of giving and being generous. He was concerned that his followers share freely, but not for the sake of impressing. He taught us to focus on him and give without fanfare. "There you are, God" (see Matthew 6:1–8).

From pizza to prayer, we make decisions about how we will live. From the secular to the sacred, we can focus on ourselves or others. Paul learned from Jesus and so can we. The best way to walk through each day is saying, "There you are," and not "Here I am!"

SHARE

What are things in our culture and the world around us that encourage a "Here I am" approach to life? What can we do as followers of Jesus to push back against these forces?

WATCH

Play the video for session two (see the streaming video access provided on the inside front cover). As you watch, use the following outline to record any thoughts, questions, or key points that stand out to you.

Two kinds of people in the world: "There you are," and, "Here I am"

Pray like it depends on God

A twofold litmus test for prayer: in the will of God and for the glory of God

Love = Grace + Truth

The Johari Window—a matrix on human personality

Quadrant 1: Arena

Quadrant 2: Façade

Quadrant 3: Blind Spot

Quadrant 4: Unknown

Seeing the image of God in other people

Some of us would rather be right than righteous

Make your prison a pulpit . . . glorify God no matter what

DISCUSS

Take a few minutes with your group members to discuss what you just watched and explore these concepts in Scripture. Use the following questions to help guide your discussion.

1. What impacted you the most as you watched Mark's teaching on Philippians 1:9–26?

2. What are some of the dangers and possible consequences of living as a "Here I am" type of person, and how does this approach to life rub against the plan of Jesus for his people? What are some of the values and blessings of living a "There you are" lifestyle, and how does this honor and bring delight to our heavenly Father?

3. **Read Philippians 1:9–11.** What are the specific elements of this prayer and what impact could God make through us if we made them a regular, consistent part of our prayer life? What is one element of this prayer that you can immediately begin lifting up for a specific person in your life? How can your group members cheer you on as you begin praying in this fresh and powerful way?

4. **Read Philippians 1:9 and John 1:14.** Give an example of extending grace but failing to speak the truth and explain how this falls short of love. Also, give an example of speaking the truth but failing to show grace and explain how this also falls short of love. How does holding to the truth *and* extending grace lead us to the deepest kind of love?

5. **Read Philippians 1:10.** What are signs that we are settling for "okay" rather than God's best and how does our culture affirm this kind of approach to life? What steps can we take to pursue God's righteousness rather than compromising or cutting corners?

6. **Read Philippians 1:12–14.** When Paul was thrown into prison for serving Jesus and preaching the good news, he was persecuted, locked up, and beaten on more than one occasion. What did God do through Paul's life as he continued to serve Jesus through those dark times? Tell about a hard time you went through and describe how God worked in you and through you during that painful season.

7. **Read Philippians 1:19–21, 25.** Consider a person in your life who needs a helping hand, a word of encouragement, or a picture of hope in a tough situation. What can you do in the next week to look at them, say, "There You Are," and help them feel the presence and care of Jesus?

MEMORIZE

Each session, you will be given a key verse (or verses) from the passage covered in the video teaching to memorize. This week, your memory verse is Philippians 1:21:

For to me, to live is Christ and to die is gain.

Have everyone recite this verse out loud. Ask for any volunteers who would like to say the verse from memory.

RESPOND

What will you take away from this session? What is one practical next step you can take from this study of Philippians 1:9–26 that will help you focus on the needs of others and serve them with humility rather than focusing on yourself?

PRAY

Close your group time by praying in any of the following directions:

- Thank God for the people in your life who have been an example of living a "There you are" life of service, compassion, and care for others.
- Ask the Holy Spirit of God to empower you to turn your focus and attention off yourself and joyfully serve, love, and care for others.
- Pray that you will be committed to serve Jesus and live for him no matter what you face and no matter how other people treat you.

SESSION TWO

Reflect on the material you have covered in this session by engaging in the following between-session learning resources. Each week, you will begin by reviewing the key verse(s) to memorize for the session. During the next five days, you will have an opportunity to read a portion of Philippians, reflect on what you learn, respond by taking action, journal some of your insights, and pray about what God has taught you. Finally, the last day, you will review the key verse(s) and reflect on what you have learned for the week.

DAY 8

Memorize: Begin this week's personal study by reciting Philippians 1:21:

For to me, to live is Christ and to die is gain.

Now try to say the verse from memory.

Reflect: Paul wrote these words from prison while he was in chains. He knew that heaven was his home and that his eternity with Jesus was secure. In light of this, he could declare that going to be with Jesus *after* this life is infinitely better than the hardships we face *in* this life. Jesus, the Good Shepherd, had left the glory of heaven and set aside his place of privilege to come and save his lost and wandering sheep. When Paul wrote, "To live is Christ," he was telling the believers in Philippi (and Christians throughout history) that pressing forward in this life and serving others is our way of becoming more like our Lord. This is following the call of Jesus to take up his cross. What are ways you can follow Jesus with increasing faithfulness, even when the road is hard?

DAY 9

Read: Philippians 1 and Philippians 1:9–11.

Reflect: How we think and the way we see the world dramatically impact how we live each day. Paul does not simply pray for love to increase. He asks God to deepen the knowledge, insight, and discernment of the Christians in Philippi. Love that is led by wisdom and insight is powerful. If we find ourselves responding to raw emotions and don't temper these feelings with wisdom and heavenly insight, we may find ourselves acting with grace but lacking truth. How can you increase your prayers for knowledge, insight, and discernment for both yourself and the Christians you care about?

Journal:
- List Christians you love and care about who need to grow in wisdom and insight as they follow Jesus?
- What specific prayers can you lift up for each of these people, and how can you encourage them to continue loving with grace but also keep growing in knowledge and discernment?

Pray: Pray for God to grant you, and people you love, increasing Spirit-led knowledge, insight, and discernment. Confess where you have operated on loving grace but lacked wisdom and insight into God's truth.

DAY 10

Read: Philippians 2 and Philippians 1:12-14.

Reflect: Your chains can unleash someone else. What a revealing passage of Scripture! Paul writes that his suffering, incarceration, and boldness to keep preaching has ignited a fire in the hearts of other believers. The gospel was advancing. Some of the believers who heard of Paul's situation began to share the good news of Jesus on their own. The guards who worked in the palace understood that Paul was wrongly imprisoned for preaching Jesus, and this made them curious about Paul's faith and the Savior he followed. Paul's chains unleashed the gospel. Are you willing to count the cost and follow Jesus, even if it costs you something? How can your willingness to follow Jesus and face hardship or persecution advance the cause of Jesus in the places God has put you?

Journal:
- What were some of the positive outcomes of Paul's very painful and negative situation?
- What are specific ways you could count the cost and pay a price for following Jesus, and how could God use your faithfulness to spread his good news right where you live, work, and play?

Pray: Ask God to give you courage to count the cost, take up the cross, and follow Jesus no matter where he leads and what the cost might be.

DAY 11

Read: Philippians 3 and Philippians 1:15–18.

Reflect: Paul makes mention of some "Here I am" people who claimed to know and follow Jesus. Try to get your mind around what was happening. Paul was in jail because of his faith and was facing serious persecution. At the same time, some Christians were trying to antagonize Paul while he could not preach. Driven by envy, rivalry, and selfish ambition, these people went out to proclaim the good news of Jesus . . . mainly to spite Paul. It seems crazy! Though their motives were corrupt, the gospel was not. Paul rejoiced that the good news of Jesus was proclaimed, even when it was done by people who were self-centered. How can you search your heart and seek to share Jesus out of good will and not selfish ambition?

Journal:
- List people you know who share Jesus with a pure heart and consistent passion. What can you learn from their example?
- What are some steps you can take to share your faith more often? What tools and learning opportunities can you use that will equip you to share faith with greater effectiveness?

Pray: Pray for the members of your small group to grow in their passion for the gospel, love for the lost, and practice of sharing their faith through the rhythms and flow of their days.

DAY 12

Read: Philippians 4 and Philippians 1:19-20.

Reflect: *Hopeful, confident,* and *trusting* . . . these words reflect the disposition of the apostle Paul while he was in a brutal situation. Through this season of persecution, he was confident that God would use even his imprisonment to bring glory to Jesus and spread his good news. When it was all said and done, Paul's deepest desire was to exalt his Savior Jesus, even if it cost his own life. What is your faith like when things seem to be going wrong, people are turning against you, and your efforts to live for Jesus seem to backfire? Do the words *hopeful, confident,* and *trusting* reflect the condition of your heart?

Journal:
- How do you tend to respond when you face deeply painful times and it feels like God is far away?
- How can you express greater faith and confidence in God during the hard times you face as a follower of Jesus?

Pray: Pray for Christians you know and care about who are going through a hard time. Ask God to give them hope, confidence, and trust that God is on the throne.

DAY 13

Read: Philippians 1:21–26.

Reflect: Paul's honest and unguarded words in this passage reveal a man who was saying "There you are." If Paul was only thinking of himself, he could have given up, stopped fighting, and just let Jesus take him home to glory. Instead, he kept pressing on, refused to give up, picked up the cross, and kept following Jesus. What motivated Paul to keep pressing on? It was the people he loved and the lost sheep who still needed to come home to Jesus. Paul's life shouted from the rooftops, "There you are!" He was all about serving others, no matter the cost. What price will you pay for others to meet Jesus and encounter the Savior who died for them?

Journal:
- Consider the people God has placed in your life so that you can help them grow and progress in their faith (i.e., family, friends, people at church, neighbors, and so on).
- What are ways you can help one or more of these people make progress in their journey *with* Jesus or *to* Jesus? What action can you take in the coming week?

Pray: Pray for personal discipline and diligence to help others grow in faith. Ask God to make this an ever-increasing passion and commitment in your life.

DAY 14

Memorize: Conclude this week's personal study by again reciting Philippians 1:21:

> For to me, to live is Christ and to die is gain.

Reflect: The incarnation of Jesus was an act of infinite sacrifice. He left the beauty of heaven for the stench of a stable. He relinquished angelic praise to hear words of rejection and denial. Jesus set aside perfect trinitarian community to feel abandonment by the Father. To live like Christ is to walk in his footsteps. What can you sacrifice as you increase your commitment to follow Jesus? It could be time, reputation, finances, or anything else you tend to hold on to. Make a choice to sacrifice something today so you can follow Jesus every day.

THE CREATIVE MINORITY

PHILIPPIANS 1:27–2:4

*Passionate followers of Jesus will always be a
minority. But such a creative and grace-driven
minority can change a community, a country,
and the world. This happens when God's people
are courageous in opposition, committed to
advancing his kingdom, directed by his Word,
and willing forgive, serve, and love others.*

WELCOME

Christians are different. Or at least we should be! If we follow
Jesus and love God with all our heart, soul, mind, and strength,
we will stand out. The majority culture around us might not
always understand Christians, but they will find our lives
compelling and attractive if we live as Jesus did.

In his book *A Creative Minority*, Jon Tyson writes these words about how followers of Jesus in the early church were dramatically different from the people around them: "The pagan society was stingy with its money and promiscuous with its body. A pagan gave nobody their money and practically gave everybody their body. And the Christians came along and gave practically nobody their body and they gave practically everybody their money."

What a powerful testimony of how Christians should look and act compared to the majority culture where God has placed us! When we show grace and kindness, but also speak truth and exemplify the way of Jesus, God moves in power.

Think about the world in the first century. Rome ruled and established peace with an iron fist and military might. There was no political or fighting force on the planet that could conquer the mighty Roman Empire. But a small group of Jesus followers who had met the Savior and lived for him whatever the cost turned Rome and the world upside down.

They forgave when assaulted. They loved when hated. They spoke truth into a world of lies. They served the marginalized when everyone else tossed them out. They prayed for those who persecuted them. They held to their faith when they were told to reject Jesus.

A small band of Jesus followers became a world movement that still exists today. We might be a minority, but if we are faithful to Jesus, he can use us to change the world in our generation.

SHARE

Tell about a time you saw (or heard about) a small group of Christians making a positive impact on a city, town, or neighborhood. Why do you think God loves to use ordinary followers of Jesus to do big things for his glory?

WATCH

Play the video for session three (see the streaming video access provided on the inside front cover). As you watch, use the following outline to record any thoughts, questions, or key points that stand out to you.

A "creative minority"

The situation in the church in Philippi

Our primary citizenship is in the kingdom of heaven

We offer a counternarrative, a counterbalance, a counterculture

A theology of dignity

A theology of equality

A theology of solidarity

The church has always been and always will be multicultural

Four things God is saying and doing in this moment:

Raising up a creative minority to reimagine the kingdom

Shifting us from a weekly rhythm to a daily rhythm

Activating the gifts of the Spirit in unprecedented ways

Decentralizing his church

Three challenges:

Play offense

Keep on keeping on

Stay humble and stay hungry

DISCUSS

Take a few minutes with your group members to discuss what you just watched and explore these concepts in Scripture. Use the following questions to help guide your discussion.

1. What impacted you the most as you watched Mark's teaching on Philippians 1:27–2:4?

2. **Read Philippians 1:27–30.** Every local church and every follower of Jesus will face growing pains, opposition, and struggles. How did the church in Philippi experience this tough reality? How are you seeing the truth of this in your church and life?

3. Respond to this statement: *If you filter your biblical theology through your political ideology, it's called idolatry!* Do you agree or disagree and why? How can Christians keep the Bible and our theology first and foremost in our lives, but still make an impact on our world around us, including the political arena?

4. **Read Philippians 1:27 and Ephesians 4:3–6.** Why is a spirit of unity and oneness so important if Christians are going to love each other and transform the world? What is getting in the way of unity in the church and what can we do to overcome these obstacles?

5. **Read Philippians 2:1–2.** Four times the apostle Paul declares, "If" in verse one. He is asking if these four things are realities in the life of Christians. Discuss each of these four statements and determine if these are realities in your life. How can you make each of these a deeper and richer reality as you follow Jesus?

6. **Read Philippians 2:3–4.** How can loving other people in the church keep our eyes on the future rather than living in the past? What are ways we can value others above ourselves and look to their interests?

7. **Read Philippians 1:28 and Matthew 7:7–8.** We are in a spiritual battle, so we need to play offense, keep on keeping on, and stay humble and hungry! What battle does your creative minority need to step into so that you can honor God and advance the cause of Jesus in your community? What step forward can you take as a small group to stand strong and fight the fight?

MEMORIZE

Each session, you will be given a key verse (or verses) from the passage covered in the video teaching to memorize. This week, your memory verse is Philippians 2:2:

> ... *Make my joy complete by being like-minded, having the same love, being one in spirit and of one mind* ...

Have everyone recite this verse out loud. Ask for any volunteers who would like to say the verse from memory.

RESPOND

What will you take away from this session? What is one practical next step you can take to mobilize the creative minority of your church to bring the love and message of Jesus to your community?

PRAY

Close your group time by praying in any of the following directions:

- As our world becomes more and more resistant to biblical truth and hostile toward committed Christians, pray for Jesus followers all over the world who are seeking to stand up as a creative and courageous minority. Lift up specific prayers for your Christian brothers and sisters in places where Christian persecution is a painful reality.
- Follow the teaching of Jesus and pray for God's kingdom to come on earth as it is in heaven. Lift up specific

places where you believe God is seeking to break in and bring his kingdom.

- Ask God to make your church (and your home) a place of dignity, equity, and solidarity.

SESSION THREE

Reflect on the material you have covered in this session by engaging in the following between-session learning resources. Each week, you will begin by reviewing the key verse(s) to memorize for the session. During the next five days, you will have an opportunity to read a portion of Philippians, reflect on what you learn, respond by taking action, journal some of your insights, and pray about what God has taught you. Finally, the last day, you will review the key verse(s) and reflect on what you have learned for the week.

DAY 15

Memorize: Begin this week's personal study by reciting Philippians 2:2:

> ... *Make my joy complete by being like-minded, having the same love, being one in spirit and of one mind* ...

Now try to say the verse from memory.

Reflect: Being like-minded does not mean all Christians think the same way. It doesn't mean we agree on everything. It certainly does not mean we all have the same tastes, interests, or passions. What it means is that we all keep our hearts and minds fixed on Jesus and we have alignment on the things that matter the most. What are some of the core beliefs that all followers of Jesus embrace and that make us distinctively Christian? How does this like-mindedness unite the family of God?

DAY 16

Read: Philippians 1 and Philippians 1:27.

Reflect: The Creative Minority of God's people in this world . . . *will conduct themselves in a worthy manner.* What does it look like to live in a manner worthy of the gospel of Jesus? The good news not only saves us from sin, but it transforms our lives. This is the journey of discipleship. It is the pathway Jesus walked. It is the road we are called to travel. What will your day look like if you seek to only do that which is worthy of the Savior who loves you and is walking side by side with you?

Journal:
- What are some of your recurring behaviors, attitudes and life patterns that are not worthy of the gospel of Jesus?

- What daily actions do you engage in that are worthy of your Savior and the price he paid to save you? How can you increase these in the rhythms of your normal day?

Pray: Ask the Holy Spirit to search your heart, mind, and motives and show you any place you are living in ways unworthy of the gospel of Jesus.

DAY 17

Read: Philippians 2 and Philippians 1:27.

Reflect: The Creative Minority of God's people in this world . . . *stand firm in the power of the Holy Spirit.* If we are going to be agents of change in this world, it will never be in our own power. The Spirit of God, who dwells within us, offers an infinite reserve of strength and energy to do what honors Jesus. We can ask for Holy Spirit power. We can stand firm in the will and ways of God's Spirit. We can unite with other

Christians in following the leading of the Spirit. How often do you pray for fresh filling and power from the Holy Spirit? Are you attentive to the whispers and nudges of the Spirit as you walk through each day?

Journal:
- In what ways do you experience the filling of God's Spirit and the power he offers?
- How can you increase your attentiveness and responsiveness to the Spirit of God when he speaks and empowers you?

Pray: Ask for renewed commitment to seek fresh filling of the Spirit and for boldness to move and act as the Spirit leads.

DAY 18

Read: Philippians 3 and Philippians 1:28.

Reflect: The Creative Minority of God's people in this world . . . *are fearless.* Paul calls the believers in Philippi to live with absolute fearlessness! We are not to be frightened in any way by people who oppose us. Any time you are part of the Creative Minority (and Christians are always in this group), there will be opposition, criticism, and sometimes persecution. No matter what we face, fear should not be our response. What pushback do you experience because of your faith and how can you grow bolder and more confident rather than letting fear creep into your heart?

Journal:
- Make a list of people and pressures you face that can come as a form of opposition to your faith in Jesus?
- What are practical ways you can resist and fight back when these people and world systems come against you?

Pray: Ask God to fill you with courage, boldness, and confidence as you face people and circumstances that seek to cause fear in your heart.

DAY 19

Read: Philippians 4 and Philippians 1:29–30.

Reflect: The Creative Minority of God's people in this world . . .
are willing to count the cost as they follow Jesus. If you read the Bible
from start to finish you will see themes that show up again and
again. One of the most consistent refrains is that living in the
will and way of God is often difficult. It costs something! Jesus
was crystal clear about this. The apostle Paul experienced it.
We will face this reality if we are serious about our faith. What
price have you paid to follow Jesus and why is it always worth
it, even when it is hard?

Journal:
- How have you suffered, been poorly treated, or paid a
  price for following Jesus?
- How has God used the hard times and seasons of suffering to grow your faith and bring you closer to his heart?

Pray: Pray for your small group members who are going
through a difficult and pain-filled time of life. Ask for God's
grace, comfort, and courage to press forward in their faith.

DAY 20

Read: Philippians 2:1–4. Read this passage slowly and reflectively, two or three times, and hear the call to an attitude of humility.

Reflect: The Creative Minority of God's people in this world . . . *are united in humble service.* Paul begins by asking if four different things are true . . . and they all are! Next, we are called to live in unity with other believers. When we know what we believe and stand unified with the church, we can take step three . . . serve with selfless humility. This is radically countercultural, but it is the call on every Jesus follower . . . living a life of humility which honors others. Does your belief in Jesus and community with his people infuse you with the confidence you need to serve others with Jesus-like humility?

Journal:
- What four things does Paul ask about in Philippians 2:1? Do you believe that each of these is true?
- What are you called to do if you affirm the four things listed in this passage? What are ways you can go deeper into the practices taught in Philippians 2:2–4?

Pray: Pray for the humility of Jesus to grow within you so that you can serve others with joy and kindness.

DAY 21

Memorize: Conclude this week's personal study by again reciting Philippians 2:2:

> *. . . Make my joy complete by being like-minded, having the same love, being one in spirit and of one mind . . .*

Reflect: The apostle Paul invites followers of Jesus to a place of deep unity and harmonious community. In this one short verse we are called to be united in thought, love, and spirit. Try to imagine a local church, a group of Christian friends, or a family that stands with their minds, hearts, and spirits in harmony. This is the way of Jesus. It is what Paul wanted for the church in Philippi and it is what Jesus wants for each of us. Where do you struggle with disunity and conflict with other believers? How can you take steps toward finding unity in these three areas of your faith? As you read, memorize, and meditate on this verse, let God draw you to deeper places of unity with your Christian brothers and sisters in your church and all over the world.

ATTITUDE CHECK

PHILIPPIANS 2:5-30

Jesus was a humble and gracious servant. He left heaven, emptied himself of divinity, lived among us, and died for our sins. When we accept the invitation to follow Jesus, we receive his grace and forgiveness. But we are also called to live as he lived, serve as he served, and love as he loved.

WELCOME

Glowing red lights on the dashboard of a car are not decorations—they are a warning. Check the oil level! Engine overheating! Electrical failure! If a light is flashing or shining for too long, the consequences can be catastrophic. In those moments, wise drivers do a system check on their car or gets it to a mechanic where a professional can make an informed assessment.

53

Imagine someone coming to you and casually saying, "I've been having sharp pains in my chest, I'm feeling weak and lightheaded, and I have discomfort in both of my arms." You ask, "How long has this been going on?" Their response is, "For three weeks, but it has gotten really bad in the past forty-eight hours!" What do you do? You get them to the hospital as fast as you can. These are classic signs of a heart attack. They need a thorough heart exam ASAP!

Your church attendance has been decreasing consistently for two years. It seems almost impossible to find volunteers for any of the church ministries. Giving is at an all-time low. Worship feels flat and there is not much joy even when singing songs with an upbeat tune and praise-focused lyrics. Any pastor, board member, or engaged church attender should be asking, "What's going on?" In a moment like this it is time to check the health of the church.

Cars need tune-ups. Bodies need check-ups. Churches need fresh vision and wise leaders who will ask the hard questions and humbly admit where things have gone off course.

What about our attitudes? How do we inspect, evaluate, and determine when our hearts have wandered from God and our attitudes needs adjustment? Some parts of the Bible act like a spotlight that shines truth into the corners of our hearts and helps us see where problems are developing. The Holy Spirit uses these inspired Scriptures to do an attitude check and get us back on the right path.

The goal of a mechanic popping the hood and inspecting an engine is not to punish the car, but to help it run at maximum capacity. A doctor does a check-up to keep the patient healthy and to help them avoid future medical problems. When a pastor gathers the church board and some gifted leaders to study the challenges they are facing, the goal is health and fresh vision for ministry. When God inspects our attitudes, it is designed to help us take fresh steps of growth and live more like Jesus.

So, pop the hood of your heart and prepare for a divine, Scripture-led attitude check. You'll be glad you did.

SHARE

Tell about a time you ignored a dashboard light, physical sign of a health problem, or a spiritual warning sign. Describe what problems developed after you looked the other way for too long.

WATCH

Play the video for session four (see the streaming video access provided on the inside front cover). As you watch, use the following outline to record any thoughts, questions, or key points that stand out to you.

Two opening observations and applications (Philippians 2:3–4):

There is no place for pride in a follower of Christ

There is no place for false humility either

Jesus is the perfect example of putting others above himself (Philippians 2:5–8)

When we choose to follow Jesus, we accept the call to be a servant

The result of Christ's incarnation and redemption

Three realms of God's sovereignty (Philippians 2:9–11):

Heaven

Earth

Under the earth

Work out your salvation with fear and trembling
(Philippians 2:12–13)

Living for Jesus is not easy, but it *is* possible (Philippians 2:14–18)

DISCUSS

Take a few minutes with your group members to discuss what
you just watched and explore these concepts in Scripture.
Use the following questions to help guide your discussion.

I. What impacted you the most as you watched Mark's teaching on Philippians 2:5–30?

2. **Read Philippians 2:3–4.** What does it mean to value others above ourselves? And what *attitudes* and *actions* show that we are living as people who place that kind of importance on each person we meet?

3. **Read Philippians 2:5–8.** Tell about a person in your life who has lived as an example of the self-sacrificing heart of Jesus. How have they served you or others and how have they inspired you to be more like Jesus?

4. Jesus was our perfect example of servanthood, sacrifice, and surrender. What are some specific occasions in his life that give us a clear picture of this reality? What will it look like in your life if you commit to follow this example of Jesus every day?

5. **Read Philippians 2:12–13.** Salvation is a gift from God received by grace. Yet, there is still a call to work hard and break a spiritual sweat. What does it look like when a committed follower of Jesus is seeking to work out their own salvation with fear and trembling?

6. **Read Philippians 2:14–18.** Pick *one* of the exhortations below and share what makes it difficult to live out. Talk about how it is possible to follow this exhortation if you walk in the power of the resurrected Savior.
    - Do all things without grumbling or complaining.
    - Become blameless and pure.
    - Be without fault in this crooked generation.
    - Hold firmly to the word of life.
    - Be glad and rejoice.

MEMORIZE

Each session, you will be given a key verse (or verses) from the passage covered in the video teaching to memorize. This week, your memory verse is Philippians 2:5:

In your relationships with one another, have the same mindset as Christ Jesus.

Have everyone recite this verse out loud. Ask for any volunteers who would like to say the verse from memory.

RESPOND

What will you take away from this session? What is one practical next step you can take to adjust your attitudes to reflect the heart and humility of Jesus?

PRAY

Close your group time by praying in any of the following directions:

- Thank Jesus for leaving heaven, emptying himself, and making a way for you to be saved and enter an eternal relationship with him.
- Invite the Holy Spirit to search your heart and do an attitude check. Pray for humility to face the areas where you need to make adjustments as you seek to live like Jesus.

- Ask God to show you where you tend to grumble, complain, and whine. Pray for the conviction of the Holy Spirit and for strength to do all things without grumbling and complaining.

SESSION FOUR

Reflect on the material you have covered in this session by engaging in the following between-session learning resources. Each week, you will begin by reviewing the key verse(s) to memorize for the session. During the next five days, you will have an opportunity to read a portion of Philippians, reflect on what you learn, respond by taking action, journal some of your insights, and pray about what God has taught you. Finally, the last day, you will review the key verse(s) and reflect on what you have learned for the week.

DAY 22

Memorize: Begin this week's personal study by reciting Philippians 2:5:

In your relationships with one another, have the same mindset as Christ Jesus.

Now try to say the verse from memory.

Reflect: Jesus is Lord of all or he is not Lord at all! Since Christians surrender every area of our lives to the Savior, we know this includes our relational world. Parents to children, and children toward parents . . . all under the leadership of Jesus. Friendships, colleagues at work, and business partners . . . each relationship should be saturated with the presence of Jesus. Marriages, sibling relationships, and how we connect with an irritating neighbor down the street . . . all of this should be surrendered to Jesus. Do you look at your relational world as the territory of Jesus' lordship? If not, what will it take to make this shift in your attitude?

DAY 23

Read: Philippians 2:5–11. Read this passage two or three times and notice the powerful example of Jesus.

Reflect: This is the great Christ hymn of the ancient church. Notice the progression downward and then upward. We begin with Jesus exalted, in very nature divine. We see an attitude of radical humility as Jesus does not cling to his rightful place and privilege. Instead, he emptied and humbled himself. He came as a man . . . in human flesh. Obedient to the Father, Jesus experienced the bitter and shameful death on a cross. He died for us, in our place, taking our shame. Then, he is exalted, lifted to the highest place, and his name is praised to the glory of the Father. How does the humility of Jesus give us a vision of how he wants us to live?

Journal:
- What do you learn about the humility and willing surrender of Jesus in this passage?
- What insight do you discover of the glory and majesty of Jesus as you hear how this song ends?

Pray: Thank Jesus for willingly leaving heaven, for humbly emptying himself, for boldly taking the cross, and for thoroughly conquering sin and hell.

DAY 24

Read: Philippians 2:12–13. Read this passage slowly and reflectively, two or three times, and hear the call to an attitude of obedience.

Reflect: *Surrender* and *obedience*. These are not popular words in our modern vocabulary. Yet this is the call of Jesus and the teaching of the apostle Paul. He reminds the Christians in Philippi that they have been obedient in the past. Now he calls them to future obedience where they work out their salvation with fear and trembling. They are to fulfill the purpose of God as they walk in his power. How can you align your desires, attitudes, and actions with God's will?

Journal:
- Consider areas of your life over the past year that you have followed God's will and grown in obedience. How have you experienced the delight of God as you have been faithful to his calling?
- Pinpoint areas that God wants to see you work to be more in line with his will. What steps can you take to surrender your desires to the will of Jesus in these areas?

Pray: Pray for power to surrender the areas of your life you tend to hold tightly and not offer to Jesus.

DAY 25

Read: Philippians 2:14–18. Read this passage three or four times and notice a whole series of attitudes that honor Jesus.

Reflect: What's wrong with a little grumbling, complaining, and whining? Everyone does it! Why is the apostle Paul calling followers of Jesus to check their grumbling spirit at the door? If you read the history of God's people as they wandered in the wilderness after the Exodus, you learn that one of their worst and repetitive sins was grumbling. They loved to do it and God hated it. It was so bad that centuries later the Paul reviewed the four big sins from the wilderness: idolatry, sexual immorality, testing God, and grumbling (see 1 Corinthians 10:6–10). Why do you think grumbling is listed among these other sins?

Journal:
- What negative consequences can come from grumbling in a home, church, or workplace?
- How can you check your attitude to ensure you are not becoming a source of grumbling in the various venues God has placed you?

Pray: Take time to confess where you have been a source of grumbling and complaining. Ask God to help you repent and turn from negative attitudes and actions.

DAY 26

Read: Philippians 2:19–24. Read this passage two or three times and pay attention to Paul's attitude about Timothy and Timothy's attitude toward the church.

Reflect: A servant, concerned for others, looking out for the interests of Jesus and his Church . . . those are the driving attitudes of Timothy. Paul was quick to celebrate this excellent example. Timothy was like a faithful son serving his father. As you read this passage, Paul's affection for Timothy is clear to see. Think of people in your life who you celebrate because they are faithful to Jesus and because they love the family of God.

Journal:
- List some of the people you see around you who are serving Jesus and his church with consistent passion and humility?
- What can you do to celebrate and bless these people as Paul honored Timothy?

Pray: Take time to pray for the people on the list you made in your journal. Ask God to bless them, continue working through them, and using them as a shining light of what it looks like to serve God's people.

DAY 27

Read: Philippians 2:25–29. Read this passage two or three times and notice Epaphroditus's attitude of self-sacrifice and hard work.

Reflect: Epaphroditus was a spiritual brother, coworker in the gospel, fellow soldier in spiritual battles, and a messenger for Jesus. Wow! What a list of qualities! Each attribute Paul mentioned comes with attitudes that make these qualities possible. Has God placed an Epaphroditus in your life? If so, do you recognize their presence and great value to the work of Jesus in the world?

Journal:
- Make a list of the numerous attributes and attitudes that marked the life of Epaphroditus. There are more than the four listed above.
- How do each of these attributes and attitudes make Epaphroditus a valuable member of God's family?

Pray: Pray that your life would be marked with the exemplary attitudes, attributes, and actions of Epaphroditus.

DAY 28

Memorize: Conclude this week's personal study by again reciting Philippians 2:5:

In your relationships with one another, have the same mindset as Christ Jesus.

Reflect: Think like Jesus! Think so much like Jesus that you act like Jesus. Act so much like Jesus that you show the Savior to the world. What will help you grow a mindset and outlook on life that is more and more like Jesus? In the coming days, actively inspect your attitudes and seek to align them with the examples of Jesus, Paul, Timothy, and Epaphroditus.

LIVE NOT BY LIES

PHILIPPIANS 3:1-21

*As we speak truth in this world, we must always
temper it with grace and love. When we live and
walk in the light of God's truth, we will put Jesus
above all else, place our confidence in him, and
press forward toward his will each and every day.*

WELCOME

The truth. Bold, clear, unfiltered.

Do you really want to hear it? Are you ready to have someone look directly into your eyes and speak the truth? Do any of us really want the people in our life (even people we love) to speak the full, unbridled, uncensored truth?

Honey, do I look like I've gained weight over the winter?

Doctor, what do the tests say?

I spent all day cooking—how does it taste?

What do I owe for my taxes?

The list could go on and on . . . and it does! At first glance it might seem that there are times we don't want to know the truth. Maybe we would prefer that someone shade the truth. Tell a little white lie. Or leave out some of the information that might sting a bit. Perhaps a half-truth would be best.

What we learn in Philippians, and many other parts of the Bible, is that speaking the truth is the right thing to do. Lying is not the path of virtue, it does not honor God, and it does not help other people.

Here is the key. Truth must be tempered by love. Truth-tellers should be guided by grace. We can speak the truth in a redemptive and life-giving way when love guides our words, tone, and motives. There is massive power when love and truth walk hand in hand.

SHARE

Tell about a time someone had the courage to speak the truth in love to you and how this impacted your life.

WATCH

Play the video for session five (see the streaming video access provided on the inside front cover). As you watch, use the following outline to record any thoughts, questions, or key points that stand out to you.

A plot line with a twist (Philippians 3:1–3)

Four ways to deal with relational conflict:

Ruinous empathy

Obnoxious aggression

Manipulative insincerity

Radical candor

The danger of adding anything to the gospel

Resumé virtues and eulogy virtues (Philippians 3:4–6)

Biblical accounting (Philippians 3:7–9)

Jesus plus nothing equals everything

Everything minus Jesus equals nothing

Becoming like Jesus—his resurrection and his suffering
(Philippians 3:10–11)

Knowing is doing and doing is knowing (Philippians 3:15–16)

Plotters and plodders (Philippians 3:17–21)

DISCUSS

Take a few minutes with your group members to discuss what you just watched and explore these concepts in Scripture. Use the following questions to help guide your discussion.

I. What impacted you the most as you watched Mark's teaching on Philippians 3:1–21?

2. What are some of the false idols and worldly ideologies that call for people in our day to bow down and worship them? How do we test cultural norms and ideologies to see if they are true and honoring to God or false and damaging to the work of his kingdom?

3. **Read Philippians 3:1-3.** Radical candor (caring deeply and confronting directly) is nothing new. It is exactly what the apostle Paul modeled on a number of occasions. How do you see Paul boldly speaking the truth while still living in grace? Share a time you exercised radical candor in a relationship. How did this affect your relationship?

What are examples of good works or behaviors some Christians feel they need to add to the gospel and why is this so dangerous

4. **Read Philippians 3:7–11 and Hebrews 12:1–3.** How does keeping our eyes on Jesus and knowing how he views us transform how we see ourselves? What has God declared to be true of you and how can you accept and walk in this reality?

5. **Read Philippians 3:12–17.** Discipleship is about observing and absorbing. Consider someone God has put in your life who is a great example of following Jesus no matter what they experience. What have you learned from being around this person? How can you stay close to people who can influence you in positive ways as you follow Jesus?

MEMORIZE

Each session, you will be given a key verse (or verses) from the passage covered in the video teaching to memorize. This week, your memory verse is Philippians 3:10:

> I want to know Christ—yes, to know the power of his resurrection and participation in his sufferings, becoming like him in his death . . .

Have everyone recite this verse out loud. Ask for any volunteers who would like to say the verse from memory.

RESPOND

What will you take away from this session? What is one practical next step you can take to speak the truth of Jesus in a gracious way with someone in your life?

PRAY

Close your group time by praying in any of the following directions:

- Give God praise for his grace which is undeserved and overflowing. Be specific about ways you have experienced grace in your life.
- Thank God for one specific person he has placed in your life who has consistently shown you what it looks like to speak the truth with bold clarity *and* with a heart filled with love. Ask God to help you learn from their example.
- Ask the Holy Spirit to fill you with courage to speak the truth with bold clarity while still loving people with growing grace.

SESSION FIVE

Reflect on the material you have covered in this session by engaging in the following between-session learning resources. Each week, you will begin by reviewing the key verse(s) to memorize for the session. During the next five days, you will have an opportunity to read a portion of Philippians, reflect on what you learn, respond by taking action, journal some of your insights, and pray about what God has taught you. Finally, the last day, you will review the key verse(s) and reflect on what you have learned for the week.

DAY 29

Memorize: Begin this week's personal study by reciting Philippians 3:10:

> *I want to know Christ—yes, to know the power of his resurrection and participation in his sufferings, becoming like him in his death . . .*

Now try to say the verse from memory.

Reflect: In this verse the apostle Paul focuses on two ways we learn to know Christ and grow in him. First, we need to know the power of his resurrection. By his might, Jesus crushed the head of Satan, destroyed death, and conquered sin. When our Savior rose from the dead, he unleashed his power in the spiritual world but also in our life. He is present. He is with us. He is alive. How can you walk with greater awareness of Jesus' presence with you now and every moment? How does the promise that one day you will rise with Jesus help you live for him each day?

DAY 30

Read: Philippians 3:1–6. Read this passage again and reflect on where you should place your confidence.

Reflect: Beware of those who place their confidence in human systems, religious regulations, and personal accomplishments. The only place to anchor our trust and allow any boasting is in Jesus Christ, who conquered sin and rose in glory. We are wise when we place our ultimate trust in Jesus and nothing else. What are ways I am placing my trust in personal accomplishments? How can I make sure Jesus is the focal point of my hope, trust, and confidence?

Journal:
- What are the accomplishments and spiritual activities that you are tempted to put your trust in and act like they make you more acceptable in God's sight?

- How can you focus your heart and life on Jesus so that you trust in him alone, and then embrace spiritual growth as a response to his amazing grace?

Pray: Pray for eyes to see where spiritual pride has taken root in your heart and pray for courage to set aside anything that has become a source of false confidence based on your own religious activity.

DAY 31

Read: Philippians 3:7–11. Read this passage two or three times and notice what Paul was willing to give up for the sake of Jesus.

Reflect: No comparison! That is what Paul is saying. Everything in this world compared to Jesus is nothing. Pile up every prize, possession, and praise from the world and Paul says you have a big heap of garbage! To be clear, the Bible is not teaching us that all these things are worthless. What we need to learn is that, next to Jesus, they all pale in comparison. If we must choose between Jesus or anything else, the reflexive response should always be obvious . . . Jesus. When you compare Jesus to the things of this world, what do you value most?

Journal:
- What are the praises, prizes, and possessions you enjoy the most in this life?
- How is Jesus better, superior, more valuable than each of these things?

Pray: Ask God to help you enjoy every good gift you have in this life, but always remember the giver of the gift is Jesus and he is worth more than all this world offers.

DAY 32

Read: Philippians 3:12–14. Read this passage three or four times and reflect on the spirit of perseverance and relentless forward movement.

Reflect: Quitting is easy. It has become a national pastime for many. When the going gets tough, cash in and watch Netflix! But God speaks into our world and hearts and calls us to press on, strain forward, and follow Jesus no matter what the cost. There is an eternal prize and heaven is real. So, until we see Jesus face to face, we are invited to strive toward all Jesus has for us in this world and after this life. What discourages you and makes you feel like giving up?

Journal:
- When have you given up, cashed in, or put your faith in neutral for a season? What caused this?
- How can you keep pressing on and continue to follow Jesus, even when times are tough?

Pray: Ask God to show you any area of your spiritual life where you have been coasting or not really pressing forward. Pray for power to fix your eyes on Jesus and keep following him with joy and passion, no matter what you face.

DAY 33

Read: Philippians 3:15–17. Read this passage two or three times and notice the call to follow good examples.

Reflect: We will all follow someone. The choice we have is who it will be. Countless groups, people, and communities invite us to join them. The advent of social media and the internet has created a place for every possible interest group and ideology to be represented. Good or bad, they are all out there. Through history, parents have known that their kids will be shaped by who they spend time with. Friends become examples and character is established through close relationships. What is true in the world is just as real in the church. With this in mind, the apostle Paul calls the Philippian Christians to follow his example and keep their eyes on people who live in a way that honors Jesus. Who do you follow and how are they influencing who you are becoming?

Journal:
- It's not just kids who are influenced by the people they hang around with. How are you being influenced (for good or bad) by the people you spend the most time with?
- What can you do to increase connections and contacts with great people who model a life of faithfulness to Jesus? How can you minimize negative influence in your life by decreasing time with people who are dragging you down spiritually?

Pray: Pray that your life and love for Jesus would be a great example for others and that people around you will become more and more like Jesus.

DAY 34

Read: Philippians 3:18–21. Read this passage two or three times and notice where we find our true citizenship and home.

Reflect: Our citizenship is in heaven. We might have a passport from the country where we are a legal citizen, but those who have received Jesus as their Savior and who follow him as Lord belong to the King, and heaven is our true and eternal home. When times are hard (don't forget, Paul is writing from a jail cell), we need to lift our eyes up from the pain of this life and remember who we are, where we are going, and fix our gaze on the One who has gone ahead of us to prepare a place. When you face hard times, where do you tend to focus your eyes and heart?

Journal:
- What are some of the best rights and privileges you have as a citizen of the country where you live?
- What are some of the rights and privileges you have as a citizen of heaven? How can you experience some of those benefits right now?

Pray: Thank God for the blessings of being a Christian and give him praise for the benefits you are experiencing now and those you will experience forever.

DAY 35

Memorize: Conclude this week's personal study by again reciting Philippians 3:10:

> *I want to know Christ—yes, to know the power of his resurrection and participation in his sufferings, becoming like him in his death . . .*

Reflect: On the first day of this week's study, we reflected on how the resurrection of Jesus helps us know him better. Today we look at the second way we get to know Jesus better. This one is less attractive but just as important. We share in his suffering! How do you get to know someone well? You experience what they have experienced. For Jesus, he faced incredible amounts of suffering as he left heaven, entered our world, lived a blameless life, died on the cross, and paid the price for our sins. As we learn about Jesus' sufferings, meditate on what he went through for us, and enter into suffering for the sake of his name, we will know Jesus more and more. What steps of faithful obedience and radical surrender can you take that just might cause you to experience suffering as you follow Jesus? What specific step will you take this week, even if it comes with some sort of suffering?

THE FOCUSING ILLUSION

PHILIPPIANS 4:1–23

What we focus on impacts our outlook, attitude, and reality. God calls us to keep our eyes, hearts, and attention on what honors him. When we do this, we learn to navigate conflict humbly, rejoice even in hard times, pray in times of anxiety, and walk in God's grace through all of our days.

WELCOME

William and Anne both love their jobs. They find their work fulfilling and each one feels like they are making a significant contribution to the world around them. Almost every morning of the first eleven months of their marriage they take a few minutes to pray for each other before heading off to work. They drive in opposite directions as they go to dramatically different worlds.

Anne works at The Old Brown Barn, a farm with chickens, cows, goats, miniature horses, and an assortment of other animals. Every day, classes from schools in the city come on field trips, and children get to pet and feed the animals. Home school groups come with parents and entire families. The kids can ride a pony for the first time, watch eggs hatch, and learn about farm life. In an orchard kids get to pick fruit and berries when they are in season and eat the freshest produce they have ever tasted. Anne gets to see the world through the eyes of children and delights in the wonder on their faces. She has half an hour drive each way and works eight full hours, but she almost always comes home with a smile on her face and stories of the children who came to The Old Brown Barn.

William heads into the heart of the city and he spends his day on a computer. He also invests his hours at work in the lives of children but in a very different way. He is on a task force that is seeking to protect children from online predators. He scours sites where children are lured by dangerous and dark people. He seeks to track down repeat offenders and stop crimes before they happen. He also must face the aftermath of the damage to children caused by these online wolves in sheep's clothing. William's eyes are focused on children all day, but there is a darkness that surrounds the work he does. As he drives home William prays and tries to shake the images and realities from his mind so that he can be fully present and engaged with his new bride when he walks in the door. He always pauses in front of the house as he parks his car on the street and quietly asks God to help him shift his focus toward what is true, noble, right, and pure. Some days this is a real challenge.

After almost a year of marriage Anne and William are still learning how to navigate their dinner conversation. They have both spent their day focusing on children, but the images, ideas, and implications of their day's work lead them to dramatically different talking points.

SHARE

How could the focus on William and Anne's day impact their dinner conversation and the way they each see the world? How can the things we focus on throughout our day shape how we see the world and ourselves?

WATCH

Play the video for session six (see the streaming video access provided on the inside front cover). As you watch, use the following outline to record any thoughts, questions, or key points that stand out to you.

Your focus determines your reality

Conflict is inevitable and unavoidable (Philippians 4:1–3)

Words matter . . . what we say and how we say it
(Philippians 4:4–5)

A remedy to anxiety . . . prayer (Philippians 4:6–7)

We need to sanctify our thoughts and fix our focus

Our ultimate focal point . . . Jesus (Philippians 4:8–9)

A challenge: start a gratitude journal

A fresh perspective on contentment and faith in God
(Philippians 4:10–20)

DISCUSS

Take a few minutes with your group members to discuss what you just watched and explore these concepts in Scripture. Use the following questions to help guide your discussion.

1. What impacted you the most as you watched Mark's teaching on Philippians 4:1–23?

2. **Read Philippians 4:5.** Tell about a time when a person spoke gentle and gracious words and how these words strengthened and blessed you.

3. **Read Philippians 4:6–7 and Matthew 5:44.** When you are hurt by someone, bothered with them, or upset by them, what do you tend to do? What is your kneejerk response (internally and externally)? How do you think your disposition and actions toward this person would change if you committed to pray for them every time you thought about the hurt you felt?

4. If you have developed *one* of these habits in your spiritual life, share how it helps you keep your focus on God and stay positive:
   ○ Keeping a written list of things you are thankful for
   ○ Reading (or listening to) the Bible each day and asking God to speak through it and teach you from it
   ○ Memorizing verses or passages from the Bible and really meditating on them.

5. **Read Philippians 4:9.** What is one lesson you have learned from the apostle Paul in this study of Philippians and how have you already put it into practice, or how will you put it into practice in the coming weeks?

6. **Read Philippians 4:13.** As we draw to the close of this study, what is one place in your life that you really need to experience the reality that you can do all things through Jesus who empowers you? How can your group members pray for God's power to be unleashed in this area of your life and how might they come alongside and walk with you through this time?

MEMORIZE

Each session, you will be given a key verse (or verses) from the passage covered in the video teaching to memorize. This week, your memory verses are Philippians 4:4–5:

> *Rejoice in the Lord always. I will say it again: Rejoice! Let your gentleness be evident to all. The Lord is near.*

Have everyone recite these verses out loud. Ask for any volunteers who would like to say the verses from memory.

RESPOND

What will you take away from this session? What is one practical next step you can do to help you shift your focus away from the things that discourage and dishearten you and focus more on Jesus than you ever have before?

PRAY

Close your group time by praying in any of the following directions:

- Ask God to help you and your group members to learn how to keep your eyes on Jesus and the things of God, even when the world is screaming for you to pay attention to everything and anything else.
- Lift up prayers of praise for things in your life and in our world that are noble, pure, excellent, and lovely.
- Lift up a prayer that is a grace note over your small group. Ask for the grace of Jesus to be with each member.

SESSION SIX

Reflect on the material you have covered in this session by engaging in the following learning resources. Begin by reviewing the key verse(s) to memorize for the session. During the next three days, you will have an opportunity to read a portion of Philippians, reflect on what you learn, respond by taking action, journal some of your insights, and pray about what God has taught you. Finally, the last day, you will review the key verse(s) and reflect on what you have learned for the week.

DAY 36

Memorize: Begin this week's personal study by reciting Philippians 4:4–5:

> *Rejoice in the Lord always. I will say it again: Rejoice! Let your gentleness be evident to all. The Lord is near.*

Now try to say these verses from memory.

Reflect: *In the Lord.* Those words are absolutely key. The apostle Paul is not saying that we should rejoice in everything that happens in life. There is deep loss, inexplicable pain, and raw evil in our world. The message is that we can rejoice "in the Lord" no matter what we face. Jesus is always with you. The Lord is near. His grace is available. Heaven is your home. God wins and Jesus is on the throne. Keep your eyes on the Lord and there will always be a reason to rejoice. When have you faced deep sorrow but still had a sense of joy deep in your heart?

DAY 37

Read: Philippians 4:1–7. Read this passage two or three times and reflect on the spirit of joy no matter what the circumstances.

Reflect: In every situation joy can be present because God is present in every situation. What is also available at all times is prayer. We can talk with God, listen for his still small voice, petition him, and give thanks to him in the darkest moments. There is no place where God won't hear our prayers. There is no time that God sleeps, slumbers, or puts his phone on "Do Not Disturb." He is always available. Why do we forget to rejoice in the Lord and talk to him in prayer in the very times we need him most?

Journal:
- When have you cried out to God amid a dark and painful time? How did God answer, show up, or bring you comfort and strength?

- When have you forgotten to cry out to God and how did this impact your journey through a hard time?

Pray: Ask God to help you keep your eyes on him in the painful and difficult times of life so that you can still find joy in him, even if the situation feels joyless.

DAY 38

Read: Philippians 4:8–9. Read this passage four or five times slowly and reflect on the things that should saturate our thinking.

Reflect: Our minds wander. We tend to focus on what is right in front of us. One of the biggest problems in this life is that the things of the world that are often a distraction yell loudly. They buzz, beep, glow, and entice us. At the same time, many of God's greatest gifts are all around us, but they are quiet, polite, and don't scream for our attention. What we need to do is slow down and notice. We can train our brain to tune in and our eyes to focus. What helps you keep your attention on the things that are good and beautiful and deserve your attention?

Journal:

- Write down at least two or three things that you think
  of in relationship to each of the words below:

  ○ What is *true* . . .

  ○ What is *noble* . . .

  ○ What is *right* . . .

  ○ What is *pure* . . .

  ○ What is *lovely* . . .

  ○ What is *admirable* . . .

  ○ What is *excellent* . . .

  ○ What is *praiseworthy* . . .

- How can you think more often and more deeply about these kinds of things?

Pray: Thank God for the beautiful, pure, and noble things around you and ask the Holy Spirit to help you notice them more often.

DAY 39

Read: Philippians 4:10–23. Read this passage two or three times and reflect on how we should view the material things God places in our care.

Reflect: Contentment in all circumstances. Generosity toward those in times of need. Fragrant offerings that bring joy to the heart of God. These things mark a Christian whose life is focused on Jesus. We are changed and no longer look, think, or act like the world around us. As we learn to focus on what honors God and means the most, we become countercultural givers who focus on the Giver far more than the gifts. How have you grown in contentment as you focus more on Jesus and live more like the Savior?

Journal:
- How has God provided and surprised you with material goods and gifts?
- How have you experienced contentment and peace, even when you did not get the material things you may have wanted?

Pray: Thank God for his amazing and lavish provision and pray that you will grow in both contentment and generosity.

DAY 40

Memorize: Conclude your forty-day personal study by again reciting Philippians 4:4–5:

Rejoice in the Lord always. I will say it again: Rejoice! Let your gentleness be evident to all. The Lord is near.

Reflect: Focus changes everything. Make time to focus on praise and thanks. Praise is worship of God for who he is: holy, powerful, tender, Shepherd, friend, comforter, and countless other attributes. Give thanks to God for what he has done for you: protection, provision, drawing near you, and so much more. Start a journal where you take time each day to write down a few declarations of praise for who God is and your prayers of thanks for what God has done.

LEADER'S GUIDE

Thank you for your willingness to lead your group through this study! What you have chosen to do is valuable and will make a great difference in the lives of others. The rewards of being a leader are different from those of participating, and we hope that as you lead you will find your own walk with Jesus deepened by this experience.

This study on Philippians in the *40 Days Through the Book* series is built around video content and small-group interaction. As the group leader, think of yourself as the host. Your job is to take care of your guests by managing the behind-the-scenes details so that when everyone arrives, they can enjoy their time together. As the leader, your role is not to answer all the questions or reteach the content—the video and study guide will do that work. Your role is to guide the experience and cultivate your group into a teaching community. This will make it a place for members to process, question, and reflect on the teaching

Before your first meeting, make sure everyone has a copy of the study guide. This will keep everyone on the same page and help the process run more smoothly. Also make sure they are aware that they have access to the videos at any time through the streaming code provided on the inside front cover. If members are unable to purchase the guide, arrange it so they can share with other members. Everyone should feel free to write in his or her study guide.

SETTING UP THE GROUP

Your group will need to determine how long you want to meet each week so you can plan your time accordingly. Generally, most groups like to meet for either sixty minutes or ninety minutes, so you could use one of the following schedules:

SECTION	60 MINUTES	90 MINUTES
WELCOME (members arrive and get settled)	5 minutes	5 minutes
SHARE (discuss one of the opening questions for the session)	5 minutes	10 minutes
READ (discuss the questions based on the Scripture reading for the session)	5 minutes	10 minutes
WATCH (watch the video teaching material together and take notes)	15 minutes	15 minutes
DISCUSS (discuss the Bible study questions based on the video teaching)	25 minutes	40 minutes
RESPOND/PRAY (reflect on the key insights, pray together, and dismiss)	5 minutes	10 minutes

As the group leader, you will want to create an environment that encourages sharing and learning. A church sanctuary or formal classroom may not be as ideal as a living room, because those locations can feel formal and less intimate. No matter what setting you choose, provide enough comfortable seating for everyone, and, if possible, arrange the seats in a semicircle so everyone can see the video easily. This will make the transition between the video and group conversation more efficient and natural.

Also, try to get to the meeting site early so you can greet participants as they arrive. Simple refreshments create a welcoming atmosphere and can be a wonderful addition to a group study. Try to take food and pet allergies into account to make your guests as comfortable as possible. You may also want to consider offering childcare to couples with children who want to attend. Finally, be sure your media technology is working properly. Managing these details up front will make the rest of your group experience flow smoothly and provide a welcoming space in which to engage the content of this study on Philippians.

STARTING THE GROUP TIME

Once everyone has arrived, it is time to begin the study. Here are some simple tips to make your group time healthy, enjoyable, and effective.

Begin the meeting with a short prayer and remind the group members to put their phones on silent. This is a way to make sure you can all be present with one another and with God. Next, give each person a few minutes to respond to the questions in the "Share" section. This won't require as much time in session one, but beginning in session two, people may need more time to share their insights from their personal studies. Usually, you won't answer the discussion questions yourself, but you should go first with the "Share" questions, answering briefly and with a reasonable amount of transparency.

At the end of session one, invite the group members to complete the "Your 40-Day Journey" for that week. Explain they can share any insights the following week before the video teaching. Let them know it's not a problem if they can't get to these activities some weeks. It will still be beneficial for them to hear from the other participants in the group. In addition, be sure the group members know that they can watch the video for the following week by accessing the streaming code found on the inside front cover of their studies.

LEADING THE DISCUSSION TIME

Now that the group is engaged, watch the video and respond with some directed small-group discussion. Encourage the group members to participate in the discussion, but make sure they know this is not mandatory for the group, so as to not make them feel pressured to come up with an answer. As the discussion progresses, follow up with comments such as, "Tell me more about that," or, "Why did you answer that way?" This will allow the group participants to deepen their reflections and invite a meaningful conversation in a nonthreatening way.

Note that you have been given multiple questions to use in each session, and you do not have to use them all or even follow them in order. Feel free to pick and choose questions based on the needs of your group or how the conversation is flowing. Also, don't be afraid of silence. Offering a question and allowing up to thirty seconds of silence is okay. This space allows people to think about how they want to respond and gives them time to do so.

As group leader, you are the boundary keeper for your group. Do not let anyone (yourself included) dominate the group time. Keep an eye out for group members who might be tempted to "attack" folks they disagree with or try to "fix" those having struggles. These kinds of behaviors can derail a group's momentum, so they need to be steered in a different direction. Model active listening and encourage everyone in your group to do the same. This will make your group time a safe space and create a positive community.

The group discussion leads to a closing time of individual reflection and prayer. Encourage the participants to review what they have learned and write down their thoughts to the "Respond" section. Close by taking a few minutes to pray as directed as a group.

Thank you again for taking the time to lead your group. You are making a difference in the lives of others and having an impact on the kingdom of God!

Study Books of the Bible with Trusted Pastors

The 40 Days Through the Book series has been designed to help believers more actively engage with God's Word. Each study encourages participants to read through one book in the New Testament at least once during the course of 40 days and provides them with:

- A clear understanding of the background and culture in which the book was written,
- Insights into key passages of Scripture, and
- Clear applications and takeaways from the particular book that participants can apply to their lives.

Available now at your favorite bookstore, or streaming video on StudyGateway.com.

ROMANS
In The Grip Of Grace
Max Lucado

MARK
The Cost Of Discipleship
Jeff Manion

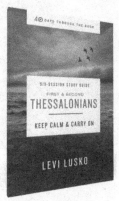

THESSALONIANS
Keep Calm & Carry On
Levi Lusko

PHILIPPIANS
Embracing Joy
Mark Batterson

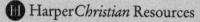